I0758366

Introduction

In today's digital world, social media plays a vital role in connecting people, businesses, and brands. Facebook (FB) and IG (IG) are two of the most popular social media platforms with millions of active users. To reach your target audience and grow your business, it's essential to understand the best practices for increasing your reach on these platforms.

In this eBook, we will be discussing strategies that A Squared, a social media marketing company, has used to help its clients increase their reach on FB and IG. Whether you're a small business owner, marketer, or content creator, these tips and tricks can help you reach more people and drive engagement on your social media accounts.

Chapter 1- Understanding your audience

The initial step to expanding your reach on Facebook and Instagram is to comprehend your target audience. Gaining a deep understanding of who your audience allows you to craft content that resonates with them, ultimately reaching a larger number of people.

To comprehend your target audience, it is essential to create a detailed avatar. This avatar should take into account three key factors: Demographics, Interests, and Behaviors.

Consider demographics such as age, gender, location, and education level. For example, if you are promoting a luxury skincare line, you might focus on an audience aged 30-50, predominantly female, with a higher education level, and living in urban areas.

One of the primary goals of a strong brand identity is to connect with your target audience on an emotional level. To achieve this, your brand identity should reflect the values and aspirations of your target audience, making it easier for them to relate to your business and feel a sense of loyalty.

Interests encompass the likes, preferences, and activities your target audience is engaged in. To illustrate, a fitness brand might target individuals who have an interest in sports, follow fitness influencers, and participate in outdoor activities.

Behaviors, on the other hand, involve the way your audience consumes content and interacts with brands. For instance, a tech-savvy audience might prefer video content over text and be more likely to engage with brands via social media or online forums.

Answering these questions will aid in developing a comprehensive avatar, allowing you to pinpoint your target audience. This understanding not only assists in communicating your objectives to your team but also helps you avoid wasting time and resources on the wrong audience. It's crucial to remember that your product or service isn't suitable for everyone. By clearly defining your audience, you save time, and money, and direct your marketing efforts more effectively.

With these basic details in place, it's time to delve deeper into the minds of your target audience. A mere understanding of who they are is insufficient; it's vital to connect with them on a deeper and more meaningful level. A refined and well- developed avatar will serve your marketing goals far better than a generic one.

Remember to ask your self these Questions! Who is your ideal customer? What are their demographics? What are their pain points and challenges? What motivates them to make a purchase?

To achieve this, ask yourself the following questions: Who is your ideal customer?

What are their demographics? (Age, gender, location, income, etc.) What are their interests and hobbies?

What are their pain points and challenges? What motivates them to make a purchase?

For instance, if you run an online coaching platform for young entrepreneurs, your ideal customer might be someone aged 20-35, with a passion for business, and struggling to scale their venture. They could be motivated to purchase by the desire to access expert advice, achieve financial freedom, or establish a successful brand.

Regardless of the nature of your venture - be it an online platform, or authoring a boo,, operating a coaching business - grasping the nuances of your target audience is crucial. Gaining a deep understanding of their needs, preferences, and expectations will enable you to tailor your content, products, or services to resonate with them on a personal level.

Gathering this information provides a well-defined target audience or avatar. With this in hand, the next step is to locate them and gather as much information about their habits and thought processes as possible. It's crucial to understand their mindset and actions intimately. As marketers, our goal is to serve our clients effectively, and the best way to do that is by comprehending our target audience's pain points and challenges.

Once you have this knowledge, you can tailor your content to address the problems and provide solutions that you already know the answers to. For example, if your audience struggles with time management and productivity, you could create content that offers tips and strategies to help them overcome these challenges, such as sharing productivity hacks, recommending time management tools, or providing case studies of successful entrepreneurs who have mastered these skills.

By developing a deep understanding of your target audience, you can create content that resonates with them, ultimately leading to a stronger connection and increased engagement. This, in turn, helps your brand gain visibility on platforms like Facebook and Instagram, as well as fosters a loyal following that is more likely to become paying customers.

The key to increasing your reach on social media platforms lies in understanding your target audience on a deeper level. By considering demographics, interests, and behaviors, as well as delving into their pain points and motivations, you can develop a comprehensive avatar that serves as a foundation for creating meaningful and resonant content. This targeted approach will not only save you time and resources but will also ensure that your marketing efforts are directed toward the right audience, maximizing your chances of success.

There are numerous methods to collect valuable information about your target audience. Consider the following approaches to gain insights into your audience's preferences, habits, and needs:

One effective way to gather data is through social media listening. This method involves using tools that monitor mentions of your brand, your competitors, and your industry across various social media platforms. For instance, a restaurant chain seeking to gauge customer reactions to their new menu items may set up a social media listening tool. This tool scans for keywords and phrases related to the brand and specific menu items, enabling the restaurant chain to identify trends and customer sentiment. By discovering that customers love the new vegetarian options but are disappointed with the seafood dish, the restaurant chain can make data-driven decisions to enhance its menu and customer experience.

Several online tools can assist you in implementing social media listening, such as Hootsuite, Brandwatch, and Talkwalker. Hootsuite offers comprehensive social media management capabilities, while Brandwatch is known for its advanced analytics.
Talkwalker, an AI-powered tool, provides real-time insights into social media activity.

Another method to obtain information directly from your target audience is by conducting surveys and questionnaires. Customer development surveys, for example, can help businesses understand their customers' needs, behaviors, and motivations. Net Promoter Score (NPS) surveys measure customer loyalty, and social media demographic surveys shed light on audience demographics such as age, gender, location, interests, and behavior. These insights enable businesses to develop targeted marketing strategies and create ads and content that resonate with their social media audience.

Competitor research is another valuable approach to gathering information about your target audience. By researching your competitors, you can gain insights into who they are targeting and how they are reaching their audience. This knowledge can help you identify opportunities and gaps in the market, enabling you to create more effective marketing campaigns.

Lastly, analyzing customer data can provide a wealth of information about your existing clientele. Understanding who is already purchasing from you and why can help you identify trends, preferences, and patterns in customer behavior. This data can be used to create content that appeals to your target audience and encourages them to interact with your brand.

Having a deep understanding of your audience's habits and preferences is crucial for creating impactful content. People tend to be creatures of habit, gravitating toward familiar places and interacting with content in consistent ways. By recognizing these patterns, you can develop content that speaks directly to your audience's needs and desires.

When creating content, always keep in mind the characteristics and habits of your target audience. Consider what type of content would resonate with them the most and strive to craft messages that cater to their preferences. By doing so, you can establish a strong connection with your audience and build a loyal following that leads to long-term success.

As you continue to engage with your audience, it is essential to adapt and refine your strategies based on the insights you gather. Regularly monitor the performance of your content to identify what works best and resonates with your target audience.

This information will help you fine-tune your marketing campaigns and make data- driven decisions that drive success.

In addition to monitoring the performance of your content, be open to experimenting with new ideas and formats. Social media platforms are constantly evolving, and staying ahead of the curve requires being flexible and innovative. For example, you might explore emerging content formats such as short-form videos, live streaming, or even virtual events to better engage with your audience and keep them interested in your brand.

Collaborating with influencers and industry experts can also contribute to your marketing efforts by providing your audience with valuable insights and fresh perspectives. By partnering with well-respected individuals in your niche, you can leverage their expertise and credibility to reach a wider audience and strengthen your brand's reputation.

Furthermore, fostering a sense of community among your followers is crucial for long- term success. Encourage interaction and engagement by responding to comments, asking for feedback, and hosting events or contests. By actively engaging with your audience and showing genuine interest in their thoughts and opinions, you can build lasting relationships and create a loyal customer base.

People tend to be creatures of habit, and understanding these habits and the places where they spend their time allows us to communicate directly with them. Consider the type of content that would be most suitable for your audience.

One option is to create personalized content that speaks directly to your target audience, addressing their pain points and challenges. For instance, a fitness brand could develop tailored workout routines or meal plans for specific demographics, such as new moms or busy professionals, ensuring the content resonates with their unique needs.

Another approach is utilizing targeted advertising to reach your audience where they spend their time online. For example, a travel company could leverage Facebook's ad-targeting features to show vacation packages to users who have recently searched for travel destinations or engaged with travel-related content.

Influencer marketing is another powerful method to reach your target audience. By partnering with influencers who have a large following within your target demographic, you can tap into their credibility and reach. A sustainable fashion brand, for example, could collaborate with an eco-conscious influencer to showcase its products, driving engagement and sales.

Additionally, customer journey mapping can help you identify opportunities to connect with your target audience at each stage of their journey. By mapping out the customer journey, you can pinpoint moments where your audience is most receptive to your message and create content that aligns with their needs. For example, a software company could offer helpful resources, such as webinars or guides, to potential customers at different stages of their research and decision-making process, ensuring that their content is relevant and timely.

In the upcoming chapter, we will delve deeper into the process of creating the ideal content for your audience. By exploring various content types and strategies, you will be better equipped to engage your target demographic and build a strong connection with them. From personalized content and targeted advertising to influencer marketing and customer journey mapping, we will guide you through the best practices for crafting compelling content that resonates with your audience and drives results. Stay tuned as we continue to uncover the secrets of successful content marketing tailored to the unique habits and preferences of your target audience.

Demographics, which include factors like age, gender, income, education, and geographic location, play an essential role in creating content that is relatable and appealing to your audience. For instance, a brand targeting young professionals might use a combination of aspirational imagery and relatable language to resonate with its audience.

Interests are another crucial element to consider when crafting content. By identifying the hobbies, preferences, and passions of your target audience, you can create content that aligns with their interests and engages them on a deeper level. For example, a clothing brand targeting eco-conscious consumers could share content about sustainable fashion practices and spotlight environmentally friendly materials.

Chapter 2: Creating Engaging Content

The subsequent step in expanding your reach on Facebook and Instagram involves crafting engaging content. To create content that resonates with your audience, there are several key aspects to consider.

Firstly, it's crucial to ensure your content is relevant to your audience and their interests. This means understanding their demographics, interests, and pain points, allowing you to create content that addresses their specific needs and preferences. Consequently, this can lead to improved engagement and increased conversions, ultimately benefiting your business.

Being visually appealing is another essential factor. High-quality images and videos can make your content stand out, grabbing your audience's attention and increasing the likelihood of interaction. For instance, a travel agency might use stunning visuals of exotic destinations to captivate its audience and inspire wanderlust.

Authenticity is also critical when sharing content on social media. Content that is true to your brand and authentic to your audience is more likely to resonate and foster genuine connections. For example, a small, family-owned bakery could share behind- the-scenes glimpses of its baking process or stories about its business's history to connect with its audience on a personal level.

Maintaining consistency by posting regularly is vital to keep your audience engaged and interested in your brand. By developing a consistent posting schedule, you can establish your brand's presence and become a reliable source of content for your audience.

To create relevant content, it's essential to research your target audience thoroughly. Understanding their demographics, interests, and pain points enables you to tailor your content to their specific needs and preferences. This research will ultimately help improve engagement and drive results for your business.

Addressing the pain points of your target audience is also essential. Pain points refer to the challenges or problems that your audience faces, such as financial stress, time management, or health issues. By providing solutions and helpful tips in your content, you can build trust and loyalty with your audience. For instance, a software company catering to small businesses could share content on how their product helps streamline workflows and save time, addressing the common pain point of time management for their audience.

In summary, crafting engaging content for Facebook and Instagram requires a thorough understanding of your target audience, along with creating visually appealing, authentic, and consistent content. By focusing on these aspects, you will be able to create content that resonates deeply with your audience and drives engagement and results for your business.

For example, a skincare brand targeting individuals with sensitive skin might share content that educates its audience on the importance of natural ingredients, while also addressing the pain points of irritation and redness. By showcasing its product's gentle and soothing properties through visually appealing images and authentic testimonials, the brand can connect with its target audience effectively.

Always remember that the key to creating engaging content on Facebook and Instagram lies in understanding your target audience's demographics, interests, and pain points. By tapping into these factors, you can tailor your content to meet their unique needs and preferences, ultimately driving engagement, building loyalty, and fostering long-lasting connections with your audience. As we continue to explore the intricacies of social media marketing, you will learn more about the strategies and techniques that will help you succeed in capturing the attention and interest of your target audience on these platforms.

In today's rapidly changing world, social media managers must remain current with events and trends to create content that captivates their audience. Here are some strategies to ensure your content stays relevant and engaging.

One approach is to follow reputable news sources and stay informed about trending topics in your industry. For example, a social media manager for a tech company could subscribe to newsletters from leading technology publications, follow news outlets on social media, or set up Google Alerts for relevant keywords. By staying informed, you can create timely, relevant content for your audience.

Another method to keep up with trends is to utilize social media analytics. By analyzing your social media posts' performance, you can identify what content resonates with your audience and discover trending topics in your industry.

Monitoring engagement rates, likes, shares, and comments can provide valuable insights. Additionally, some social media platforms like Twitter have a trending topics section, which can be useful for staying informed about current news.

Engaging with industry groups and forums is another way to stay current on events and trends. This engagement allows you to connect with other professionals in your industry, exchange knowledge, and remain informed about the latest news and trends. Platforms like LinkedIn offer industry groups, while resources like Reddit and Quora provide access to industry forums.

Tap Into Industry Forums

Attending industry events and conferences is an excellent opportunity to stay up to date on the latest trends and network with other professionals. For instance, a social media manager in the marketing industry could attend a digital marketing conference, where they would learn from experts, gain new insights, and stay informed about the latest news and developments in the field.

Utilizing content aggregators like Feedly and Flipboard can also help you stay informed about current events and trends. These platforms allow you to curate content from multiple sources and customize your feed based on your interests. As a result, you can stay informed about the latest news and trends in your industry, which enables you to create timely and relevant content for your social media channels.

Staying informed about current events and trends is crucial for social media managers looking to create content that connects with their audience. By following news sources and trending topics, using social media analytics, participating in industry groups and forums, attending events and conferences, and employing content aggregators, you can stay updated on the latest news and trends in your industry. With this knowledge, you can develop content that engages your audience and keeps them coming back for more.

Emphasizing your brand's Unique Value Proposition (UVP) is critical in today's competitive landscape. A UVP is a succinct statement that conveys what distinguishes your brand from others in the market. To ensure your target audience understands your UVP, consider the following strategies:

First, pinpoint your unique selling point (USP), which sets your brand apart from competitors. This can be done by analyzing your brand's strengths and weaknesses, identifying market gaps, and understanding the needs and pain points of your target audience. Your USP should be unique, valuable, and relevant to your audience.

Communicate your USP through clear and concise messaging that is easy to understand and memorable. Achieve this by using simple language, clear messaging, and consistent branding across all marketing channels, such as Facebook, Instagram, Twitter, Pinterest, LinkedIn, YouTube, and TikTok. Each of these platforms serves different purposes and caters to various audiences, making them ideal for showcasing your brand's unique features in a variety of ways.

Develop a compelling value proposition statement to convey your UVP to your target audience. This statement should clearly express what sets your brand apart, the value you offer, and the advantages of choosing your brand over others. Include this statement on your website, social media channels, and other marketing materials.

Highlight your brand's UVP by leveraging customer testimonials and reviews. This social proof can effectively demonstrate the value and benefits of choosing your brand over others. For instance, a company like Warby Parker, known for its affordable and stylish eyewear, showcases customer reviews on its website and social media channels to emphasize its UVP of providing a seamless, affordable, and fashionable eyewear experience.

Showcase your unique brand personality as another way to emphasize your UVP. Develop an authentic, relatable brand personality that aligns with your target audience's values and preferences. For example, outdoor gear company Patagonia effectively showcases its commitment to environmental sustainability through its marketing materials, social media channels, and customer interactions. By taking a clear stance on environmental issues and supporting related causes, Patagonia has created a unique brand personality that resonates with its eco-conscious audience.

Highlighting your brand's unique value proposition is crucial for standing out in a competitive market. By identifying your unique selling point, using clear and concise messaging, creating a compelling value proposition statement, leveraging customer testimonials and reviews, and showcasing your unique brand personality, you can effectively communicate your UVP to your target audience and differentiate your brand from others in the market. Real-life examples, like Warby Parker's customer reviews and Patagonia's eco-friendly brand personality, demonstrate the power of effectively showcasing a brand's unique value proposition.

Another real-life example is Apple, which highlights its UVP through sleek design, innovation, and user experience. Apple consistently communicates its commitment to creating cutting-edge technology that is both functional and aesthetically pleasing.
By showcasing these features across its marketing materials, website, and social media channels, Apple has built a loyal customer base that values its distinct offerings.

In the case of Airbnb, the company has successfully differentiated itself by promoting a unique travel experience that goes beyond traditional hotel accommodations.

Airbnb emphasizes its UVP of providing authentic, local experiences by showcasing real homes and diverse hosting options, while also highlighting the connections between hosts and guests. By sharing stories of these unique experiences on their website and social media channels, Airbnb has managed to create a brand that resonates with travelers seeking an alternative to conventional accommodations.

These examples illustrate the importance of effectively communicating your brand's unique value proposition to your target audience. By doing so, you not only differentiate your brand from competitors but also build trust and loyalty among your customers. Ultimately, a well-defined and communicated UVP can lead to increased brand awareness, customer engagement, and long-term success.

Let's Talk about Visually Appealing Content!

So let's talk about creating Visually Appealing Content!

In today's fast-paced world, capturing your audience's attention is more important than ever. One way to achieve this is by making your content visually appealing. High-quality images, videos, and graphics can help your content stand out and engage your target audience. Let's explore some strategies for crafting visually stunning content.

The first step to creating visually appealing content is investing in high-quality images and videos. A prime example of a brand that leverages high-quality visuals to enhance engagement is Airbnb, which uses professional photography for its property listings. This not only makes the listings more attractive but also instills a sense of trust in potential guests.

Another essential aspect of creating visually appealing content is using eye-catching graphics and design elements. Apple is a brand that excels in this area, consistently producing sleek, minimalist graphics that complement its products and overall branding.

In addition to images and graphics, utilizing Instagram's features is an excellent way to showcase your brand in an aesthetically pleasing manner. Instagram offers a variety of tools such as Stories, Reels, and IGTV, which we will discuss in more detail later in the book.

Now that you understand the importance of visually appealing content, let's examine how to invest in quality images and videos. First and foremost, determine your budget and goals for acquiring high-quality visuals. This will help you identify the type and quality of images and videos you need and where to find them. Setting a budget that aligns with your business's needs and goals is essential.

Once you have a budget and goals in place, create a brief for the visuals you require. This brief should include details on the style, format, resolution, and any specific requirements you may have. By clearly communicating your needs, you can ensure that potential vendors deliver a final product that meets your expectations.

One option to consider when sourcing high-quality visuals is hiring a professional photographer or videographer. Companies like A Squared specialize in creating custom visuals that align with your brand's style and goals. You can find other professionals on freelance websites such as Upwork, Fiverr, and Freelancer, or by searching for local professionals on social media platforms like LinkedIn or Instagram. Remember to review their portfolios and make sure their style and quality align with your needs and goals.

Purchasing stock images and videos is another viable option. Reputable online sources like Shutterstock, iStock, and Adobe Stock offer a wide range of pre-shot images and videos that can be licensed for use in your marketing materials. These websites allow you to search for visuals by keyword or category, making it easy to find the perfect fit for your content.

Alternatively, you can utilize free image and video resources available online. Websites like Unsplash, Pexels, and Pixabay offer high-quality images and videos that can be used for commercial purposes without any cost. However, it's crucial to read and follow the licensing terms for each image or video to avoid any legal issues.

By determining your budget and goals, creating a brief, hiring a professional photographer or videographer, purchasing stock images and videos, or using free image and video resources, you can find high-quality visuals that align with your brand's style and goals. This investment can help your brand stand out in a crowded marketplace and ultimately drive business success.

In summary, crafting visually appealing content is a vital aspect of capturing your audience's attention and differentiating your brand in today's competitive landscape. High-quality images, videos, and graphics can significantly impact engagement and reach, ultimately contributing to your business's growth. By following the strategies outlined in this section, you can create visually stunning content that will resonate with your target audience and elevate your brand.

Visual content is a powerful tool for capturing attention and leaving a lasting impression on your audience. By incorporating eye-catching graphics and design elements, you can ensure that your content stands out and resonates with your target demographic. In this section, we will explore various techniques to enhance your visual content, offering real-life examples and practical tips for success.

First and foremost, it's essential to establish your branding guidelines. These guidelines will dictate the consistency of your graphics and design elements, aligning with your brand's voice and style. Your branding guidelines should encompass your color palette, font selection, and overall graphic style. A solid foundation in branding will enable you to create cohesive visuals that accurately represent your brand.

High-quality images are a cornerstone of visually appealing content. Aim for high- resolution, well-lit images that are sharp and clear. Steer clear of low-quality, blurry, or pixelated visuals, which detract from your message. To source high-quality images that align with your brand, consider stock image websites such as Shutterstock, iStock, and Adobe Stock.

Infographics serve as an effective means of conveying complex information in a visually engaging manner. By combining text, images, and data, infographics present information clearly and compellingly. Online tools like Canva, Piktochart, and Venngage empower you to create customized infographics that align with your brand's style. Canva, for instance, is a popular editing app offering a free account with access to graphics, videos, and stock footage. Upgrading to a paid version unlocks a vast catalog of additional content to elevate your visual storytelling.

Video content offers an excellent medium for engaging your audience and delivering your message. Use videos to showcase products, demonstrate services, or provide educational content. Tools like Adobe Premiere, iMovie, and Final Cut Pro can help you edit and create high-quality video content. For example, a small business owner might use iMovie to create a video tutorial demonstrating the features of their latest product.

Incorporating animations and GIFs into your content adds visual interest and can enhance your message. These dynamic elements can highlight product features, inject humor, or provide visual cues. Tools such as Canva, Adobe After Effects, Procreate, and Animate enable you to create custom animations and GIFs that match your brand's style. A marketing campaign, for example, might use an animated GIF to showcase the ease of using a new mobile app.

While it's crucial to create visually appealing content, simplicity should not be overlooked. Avoid overwhelming your audience with cluttered designs, and instead, opt for a limited color palette and one or two primary design elements. This approach will help your audience focus on your message and ultimately increase engagement.

Leveraging eye-catching graphics and design elements can significantly enhance the visual appeal and engagement of your content. By adhering to your branding guidelines, using high-quality images, incorporating infographics, integrating video content, employing animations and GIFs, and maintaining simplicity, you can create visually captivating content that accurately represents your brand and drives business success.

Instagram (IG) has revolutionized the way businesses connect with their target audience and promote their brand. As a powerful social media platform, IG boasts a plethora of features designed to help you create eye-catching graphics that captivate your followers. In this section, we will explore various tips and techniques to make the most of IG's features for stunning visual content.

One of the most popular features on IG is Stories, which allows users to share eye- catching graphics that disappear after 24 hours. This ephemeral nature encourages users to post casual, spontaneous, and genuine moments, fostering a more authentic experience. For instance, a local bakery might use Stories to share the day's specials, a sneak peek of a new pastry in the works or even a glimpse into the baking process. By incorporating stickers, GIFs, and filters, your Stories will stand out and engage your audience.

Stories' fleeting nature offers several advantages, such as motivating users to post content more frequently and promoting real-time interactions between users and their followers. As a result, IG becomes a dynamic space where users can share their lives as they unfold. Moreover, Stories help alleviate the pressure of producing high-quality content, allowing users to share candid moments without needing to adhere to a specific aesthetic or theme for their main feed.

Another powerful feature is Instagram Reels, which lets users create and share short- form video content. For example, a fitness instructor might use Reels to showcase a quick workout routine, set to an upbeat soundtrack, and accompanied by text overlays to explain each exercise. By experimenting with music, filters, and overlays, your Reels will captivate your audience and showcase your products or services.

To further enhance your graphics, make use of IG's editing tools. Adjust the brightness, contrast, and saturation of your images, and explore built-in filters to create a unique look and feel. Consider the transformation of a simple travel photo into an evocative, vibrant image that transports your audience to the destination.

Maintaining consistency across your IG content is crucial, and custom templates can help. Tools like Canva, Adobe Spark, and PicMonkey enable you to create templates that align with your branding guidelines, streamlining the creation process for everything from Stories to Reels.

Hashtags and captions play a vital role in expanding the reach of your IG graphics. By incorporating relevant hashtags, you increase the likelihood of discovery by a wider audience. For instance, a vegan restaurant might use hashtags such as #veganfood or #plantbased to attract potential customers. Additionally, crafting compelling captions can make your graphics more engaging and inspire your audience to take action.

Lastly, don't shy away from experimenting with different formats when creating IG graphics. Explore carousels, collages, and multiple images to add visual interest and variety. A fashion retailer, for example, might create a carousel featuring a model wearing their latest collection, allowing followers to swipe through multiple outfits in one post.

In summary, Instagram offers a wealth of features to create eye-catching graphics for your business. By harnessing the power of Stories and Reels, utilizing IG's editing tools, crafting custom templates, leveraging hashtags and captions, and experimenting with various formats, you can develop compelling visuals that captivate your audience and boost engagement for your brand.

Authenticity: The Key to Lasting Engagement

In the realm of content creation, visual appeal is undoubtedly important. However, focusing solely on aesthetics can cause creators to overlook other vital aspects of connecting with their audience. The secret to crafting engaging and enduring content lies in authenticity.

A question I once encountered was, "How do you show authenticity without losing authenticity?" Initially perplexed, I realized that the person was concerned that their genuine content might be perceived as fake. The desire to project perfection often hinders people from creating authentic content, fearing it might drive their audience away or be dismissed as insincere. However, the key is to remember that audiences crave authenticity, particularly in a world saturated with over-marketed sales pitches.

Being authentic simply means being yourself. As people increasingly seek genuine connections online, sharing authentic images, videos, and posts can significantly boost engagement and followers. Authentic content allows audiences to see the real person behind the screen, breaking down the barriers created by the often superficial nature of social media. When users share candid moments, unfiltered emotions, and raw experiences, it fosters a deeper connection with their audience, leading to trust, loyalty, and active engagement.

Genuine content also sparks meaningful conversations and interactions, as people feel more inclined to comment on and share relatable posts. By creating a space for open dialogue and discussion, authentic content cultivates a sense of community among followers, boosting engagement, and organically expanding their social media following.

Furthermore, the constant exposure to perfectly curated feeds and meticulously crafted images can be exhausting. Authentic content offers a refreshing break from polished posts, appealing to those seeking a more genuine representation of life.
Sharing content that reflects the user's true personality, interests, and experiences attracts followers who appreciate this sincerity and are more likely to engage with their posts.

Additionally, creating and sharing authentic content can be both enjoyable and fulfilling for the user. By being true to themselves and their audience, users can develop their unique voice and personal brand, standing out from the competition and attracting a following that appreciates their distinct perspective.

Here are some tips for creating authentic content:

Be transparent: Share behind-the-scenes content and offer a glimpse into your brand's personality and values. For instance, a fashion designer could share a video of their creative process or a photoshoot's backstage moments.

Highlight your brand's unique story: Share the story of your brand and what sets you apart from the competition. A small, family-owned business might emphasize its commitment to community involvement or its dedication to preserving traditional craftsmanship.

Encourage user-generated content: Foster a sense of community and engagement by actively encouraging your audience to share their personal experiences and content related to your brand. Companies can create and promote branded hashtags, launch social media contests or challenges, or collaborate with influencers and brand ambassadors.

Showcase user-generated content: Feature customer stories, testimonials, or images on your social media channels, website, or marketing materials. This not only validates the customer's experience but also serves as a powerful form of social proof, attracting new customers who seek authenticity in their brand interactions.

Engage with your audience: Actively engage with your audience by responding to comments, reposting user-generated content, and expressing gratitude for their support. By maintaining open communication and acknowledging the value of user- generated content, companies can create a loyal, engaged, and passionate community around their brand.

Authentic images, videos, and social media posts are the cornerstone of building a loyal and engaged following. By embracing authenticity, creators can forge genuine connections with their audience, boost engagement, and establish a strong personal brand that stands out in the ever-evolving world of social media.

Creating Transparent Content: The Key to Trust and Authenticity

Creating transparent content is essential for building strong relationships with your audience and promoting a culture of honesty and openness. When you produce content that is open and genuine, you establish trust and authenticity with your followers, which ultimately drives business success.

To create transparent content, start by being honest and authentic. Open up about your business practices, goals, and challenges. Demonstrating transparency helps you build trust with your audience and cultivate a sense of authenticity that resonates with your followers.

Sharing your story is another effective method of creating transparent content. This involves discussing your background, values, and mission. By doing so, you enable your audience to connect with your brand on a deeper level and create a sense of community around your brand.

Offering insights and data can also promote transparency. Share your business performance, customer feedback, and growth strategies with your audience. This information gives them a clear understanding of your business practices and showcases your commitment to openness and honesty.

It's important to acknowledge that no business is perfect. Addressing mistakes and challenges is a crucial aspect of creating transparent content. When you acknowledge and address errors, you demonstrate your commitment to accountability, fostering a sense of trust with your audience. Moreover, it provides opportunities for improvement and growth.

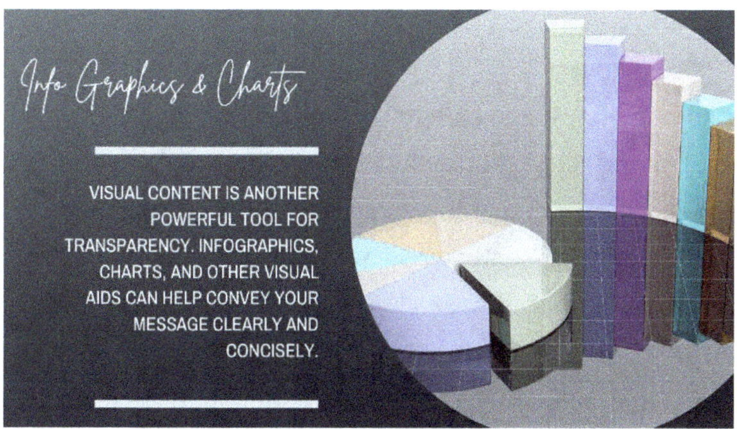

Visual content is another powerful tool for transparency. Infographics, charts, and other visual aids can help convey your message clearly and concisely. Authentic images and videos also contribute to building a sense of transparency and authenticity around your brand.

Encouraging feedback and discussion is a key element of creating transparent content. By fostering an open dialogue with your audience, you can gain valuable insights, address concerns, and create a sense of community around your brand. Invite your audience to share their thoughts and ideas, and respond to their feedback openly and honestly.

Consistency is crucial for maintaining trust and authenticity. If you don't post regularly, your social media page may lack the content necessary to establish trust. Imagine visiting a brick-and-mortar store with only one or two items on empty shelves – you'd likely question the store's legitimacy. The same principle applies to a sparse social media page. A mostly empty page with only sales pitches or random product images will make it difficult for visitors to trust the content.

By being honest and authentic, sharing your story, offering insights and data, addressing mistakes and challenges, using engaging visuals, and encouraging feedback and discussion consistently, you can create a culture of transparency that resonates with your audience and drives business success. Transparency fosters trust and a sense of connection, allowing your brand to flourish in the digital landscape.

That is why…

Consistency: The Cornerstone of Social Media Success

Consistency in posting is essential for keeping your audience engaged and building a strong social media following. To stay consistent, consider the following strategies:

Create a content calendar:

Planning your content ensures that you maintain a regular posting schedule. Define your goals, target audience, and channels to identify the best topics and themes for your content. Use a content calendar template to outline your content ideas and develop a posting schedule for the upcoming weeks or months.

Utilize automation tools:

Automation tools, such as Hootsuite, Buffer, and Sprout Social, can streamline your content creation and posting process. By scheduling your posts in advance, you can maintain a consistent posting schedule even during busy periods.

Experiment with different types of content:

To keep your audience engaged and prevent boredom, mix up your content. Experiment with various formats, such as videos, infographics, or articles, to identify what resonates best with your followers.

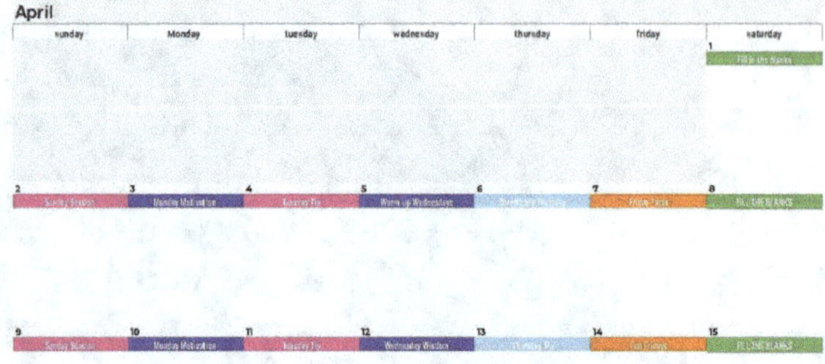

Creating a content calendar may initially seem daunting, but by defining your goals and target audience, identifying relevant channels, brainstorming content ideas, and monitoring analytics, you can successfully plan your content and maintain a consistent posting schedule.

Automation tools can further enhance your social media strategy by saving you time and ensuring your content is consistent. However, while these tools are valuable, they shouldn't replace personal interactions with your audience. Regularly engage with your followers by responding to comments and messages to foster a sense of community and connection.

Finally, experimenting with different types of content helps you stay on top of trends, better understand your audience, and keep your content fresh and engaging. By identifying which content formats work best for your brand, you can optimize your social media strategy and drive better results.

By creating a content calendar, utilizing automation tools, and experimenting with different content types, you can achieve consistency in your social media strategy, ensuring your audience remains engaged and helping your brand thrive in the digital landscape.

Maintaining Consistency and Diversifying Content for Success:

Consistent posting is essential for engaging your audience and building a robust following on social media. To ensure you post regularly, it's crucial to create a content calendar, utilize automation tools, and experiment with diverse types of content.

Creating a content calendar might initially seem overwhelming, but by following a few simple steps, you can plan your content efficiently. Start by defining your goals and target audience. Knowing your target audience and their interests will help you produce content that resonates with them and achieves your objectives. These questions should already have been addressed if you've followed the steps outlined earlier in the book.

Next, identify the channels for content distribution and the frequency of your posts. Popular channels include social media, blog articles, email newsletters, and video content. The frequency of your posts will depend on your goals and chosen channels. It's essential to find a frequency that works for your business and helps you achieve your goals. Generally, posting a minimum of three times a week keeps your content fresh and relevant.

Once you've identified your goals, target audience, and channels, brainstorm content ideas. Consider topics and themes relevant to your audience and goals, and think about the types of content that will resonate with them and drive engagement. You can also use keyword research and industry trends to inform your content ideas.

Create a content calendar template that includes the date, channel, content type, topic, and any other relevant details. You can use a spreadsheet, or specialized tools like the Free FB Meta Suite, Hootsuite, or CoSchedule. Alternatively, you can use a third-party calendar to plan your content. With your template in hand, begin filling in your content calendar, and creating a schedule of posts and content for the upcoming weeks or months. Make sure to leave room for flexibility and adjust your calendar as needed.

Chapter 3: Optimizing Your FB and Instagram Profiles

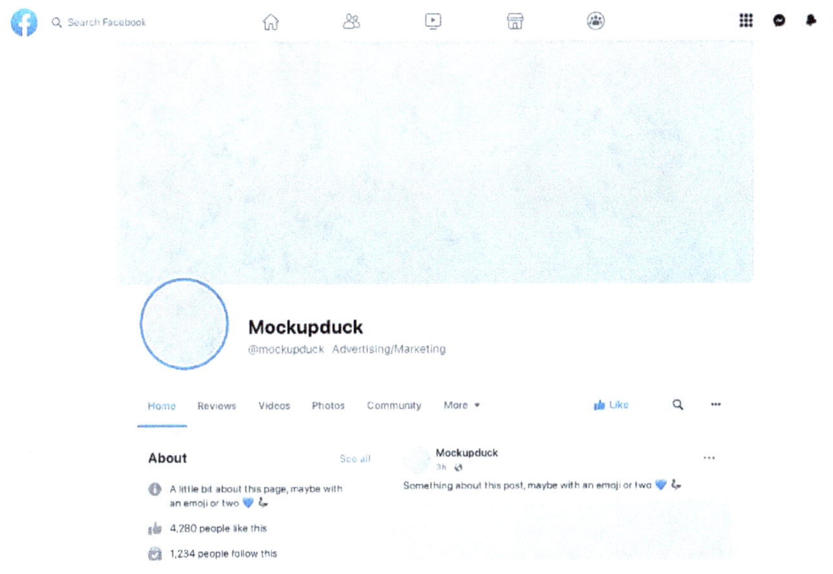

Optimizing your Facebook and Instagram profiles is essential for increasing your reach and making a powerful impact on your target audience. There are several key aspects to focus on when optimizing your profiles, such as your profile picture, bio, links, and contact information.

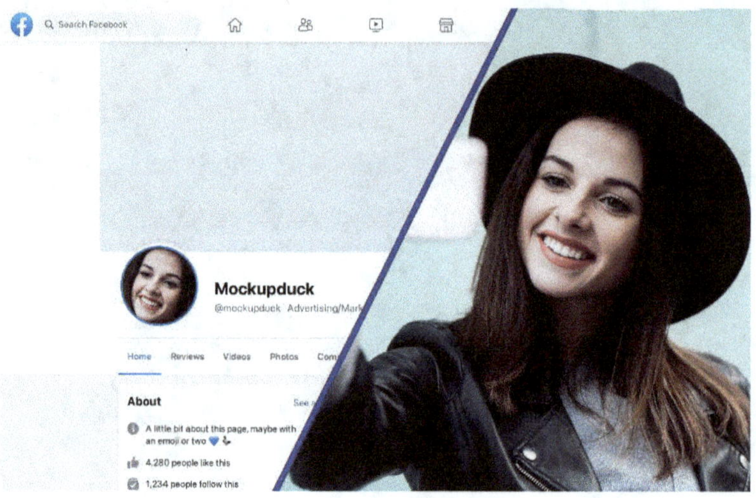

A high-quality profile picture that accurately represents your brand is crucial for creating a strong first impression. For instance, Apple's profile picture on both Facebook and Instagram features their well-known logo, ensuring consistency and instant recognition. When selecting the perfect profile picture, consider the following tips:

When your content calendar is ready, plan by creating content in advance and scheduling it for future publication. This approach helps you stay on track and ensures a steady stream of content for your audience. Regularly analyze your content calendar, using analytics and metrics to measure the success of your content, and adjust your strategy accordingly.

With a content calendar in place, consider automation to streamline your content creation and posting process. Before using automation tools, define your goals and objectives to select the right tools and create a plan aligned with your goals. Common social media goals include increasing engagement, driving website traffic, and generating leads.

Hootsuite   Sproutsocial   Buffer

Social Media Automation Tools

Several social media automation tools are available, such as Hootsuite, Buffer, and Sprout Social. For those focusing on Facebook and Instagram, the Meta Business Suite, created by Meta (formerly Facebook), is a free platform that allows you to post to both channels. When selecting tools, consider your budget, required features, and the social media platforms you are active on.

Automation tools are most effective when you have a clear content plan. Use your content calendar to plan social media posts, including topics, images, and captions. Automation tools can then schedule your posts, saving you time and ensuring consistency. While these tools save time, it's still crucial to monitor and analyze your results, adjusting your strategy and optimizing your posts accordingly. Automation tools shouldn't replace personal interactions with your audience, so regularly monitor your social media accounts and engage with your audience by responding to comments and messages.

One potential pitfall of automation is the risk of content becoming stale due to consistent planning. To mitigate this, it's essential to experiment with different types of content. Experimenting can help you understand your audience and what resonates with them. By testing various content types, you can identify which receives the most engagement, generate leads, or drive website traffic. This information helps optimize your social media strategy and create more effective content.

Diversifying your content also helps prevent stagnation and keeps your audience engaged. Repeatedly posting the same types of content may bore or disengage your audience. By introducing new content formats, such as videos or infographics, you can maintain your audience's interest and encourage them to continue following your brand.

Experimenting with different types of content allows you to stay on top of trends and changes in the social media landscape. As new platforms emerge and existing ones introduce new features, new content formats may gain popularity or become more effective. By exploring new content types, you can stay ahead of the curve and capitalize on new opportunities.

For example, consider the rise of TikTok, which has gained immense popularity due to its short-form video content. Brands that quickly adapted to this new format and platform saw increased engagement and reach. Another example is Instagram's introduction of Reels, which presented an opportunity for brands to create short, engaging videos to reach a broader audience.

Choose an image that reflects your brand: Your profile picture should visually represent your brand identity. Make sure the image aligns with your brand's colors, tone, and message. For example, Coca-Cola's profile picture features its iconic logo, emphasizing the brand's colors and style.

Use high-quality images: A pixelated or blurry profile picture can deter potential followers or customers. Ensure your image is high-quality and sharp, with a resolution of at least 180x180 pixels on Facebook and 110x110 pixels on Instagram.

Keep it simple: Your profile picture should be easily recognizable and distinguishable from other images. Avoid cluttered images or those with excessive text. A clean and straightforward image, such as Google's simple multicolored "G" logo, is more memorable and identifiable.

Test different images: Don't hesitate to experiment with various profile pictures to determine which resonates best with your audience. Monitor engagement metrics using Facebook or Instagram Insights to gauge which images perform the best.

Be consistent: Once you've chosen a profile picture, maintain consistency across all your social media profiles to establish brand recognition and increase brand awareness.

In addition to a great profile picture, crafting an engaging and concise bio is vital for effectively describing your brand and what you do. For example, Netflix's Instagram bio reads, "Movies, TV shows, and all things streaming. Your daily source for what to watch .." To write an impactful bio, identify your brand's key message, maintain brevity, use relevant keywords, showcase your personality, and update it regularly.

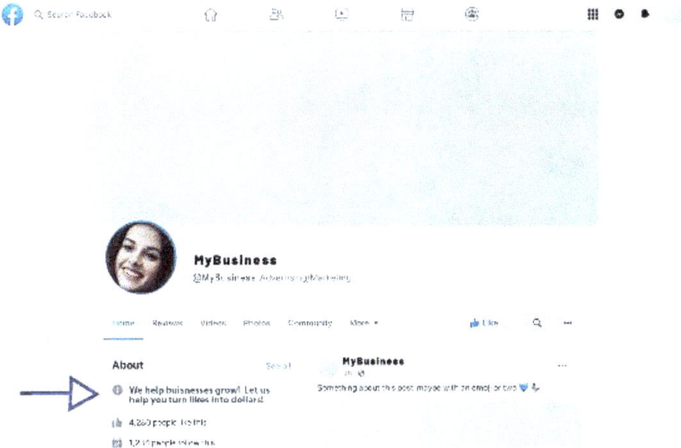

Incorporating links to your website, blog, or other social media accounts in your bio is another critical element of optimization. This allows followers and potential customers to access more information about your brand, products, or services easily.

For instance, National Geographic's Instagram bio contains a link to its latest articles and features. To optimize your links, prioritize the most important ones, use shortened links, emphasize your call-to-action, and ensure your links are up-to-date.

In conclusion, consistency and diversifying your content are crucial for building an effective social media strategy. By creating a content calendar, utilizing automation tools, and experimenting with different types of content, you can maintain a social media presence that drives results and keeps your audience engaged. Remember to monitor your results, adjust your strategy as needed, and stay up-to-date with trends to ensure your content remains fresh, relevant, and appealing to your target audience.

Lastly, providing contact information on your profiles enables your audience to reach you effortlessly. For example, the popular restaurant chain Chipotle includes their email address, phone number, and a "Contact Us" button on their Facebook page, simplifying communication for customers. To optimize contact information, include your email address, phone number, a contact button, and a link to your website's contact page, and respond to inquiries promptly.

In summary, optimizing your Facebook and Instagram profiles is a vital aspect of your social media marketing strategy. By concentrating on your profile picture, bio, links, and contact information, you can create a strong and lasting impression on your target audience, ultimately driving traffic to your website and fostering engagement with your brand. Regular updates and consistency across platforms will help maintain a professional and trustworthy online presence.

identifying your brand's key message is a crucial first step in crafting an engaging and informative bio for your Facebook and Instagram profiles. Determining what sets your brand apart from competitors and what unique offerings you provide will help you create a bio that showcases your value proposition. For example, Tesla's Instagram bio highlights its mission to accelerate the world's transition to sustainable energy, clearly communicating its key message and setting them apart from traditional automobile companies.

Keeping your bio concise while still conveying your message effectively can be challenging. Aim for a bio that is no longer than 150 characters and focuses on your key message. Avoiding unnecessary jargon or complicated language will help maintain clarity and prevent confusion or disinterest among your audience. For instance, Starbucks uses a short and sweet bio on their Instagram account: "Inspiring and nurturing the human spirit—one person, one cup, and one neighborhood at a time."

Incorporating relevant keywords can improve your visibility in search results, making it easier for your target audience to find your brand. Consider the terms and phrases your audience might use when searching for brands like yours, and weave them into your bio naturally. For example, a fitness trainer might include keywords like "personal training," "workout routines," and "nutrition tips" in their bio.

Showing some personality in your bio can make your brand more relatable and engaging. Maintain a tone and voice consistent with your brand's overall image, but don't be afraid to add a touch of humor or personal flair. Mailchimp's Instagram bio, for example, maintains a playful tone: "Marketing smarts for big ideas. We make it easy to help you grow, with all the tools you need to level up your business."

Regularly updating your bio ensures it stays current and accurately reflects your brand. Changes in your business, product offerings, or promotions might necessitate bio updates, so stay vigilant and keep your bio fresh.

Including links in your Facebook and Instagram bios is an effective way to optimize your profiles and direct traffic to your website, blog, or other social media accounts. Prioritize your most important links, such as your homepage or a specific landing page, and use URL shorteners like Bitly or Ow.ly to create cleaner, more readable links. Including a clear call-to-action, like "Shop our latest collection" or "Visit our blog for inspiration," encourages users to engage with your content.

Instagram's "swipe up" feature, available to business accounts with over 10,000 followers, allows you to include clickable links in your Stories. This feature is an excellent way to promote specific products, blog posts, or other content to your audience.

*Swipe Up for accounts with more than **10,000** followers*

Regularly checking and updating your links ensures they remain functional and relevant, providing a seamless experience for your followers.

Providing contact information on your Facebook and Instagram profiles simplifies communication for your followers and potential customers. Include your email address, phone number, and a contact button with a customized call-to-action, like "Contact Us" or "Get in Touch." Linking to your website's contact page offers another avenue for users to connect with you.

Prompt and professional responses to inquiries can help build trust and foster positive relationships with your audience. Regularly checking your inbox and responding to messages promptly demonstrates your commitment to customer satisfaction.

In conclusion, optimizing your Facebook and Instagram profiles is a critical component of your social media marketing strategy. By focusing on your bio, links, and contact information, you can create an engaging and informative experience for your followers, driving traffic to your website and promoting positive interactions with your brand.

Chapter 4: Utilizing Hashtags and Tagging

Hashtags and tagging are indeed essential tools for expanding your reach on Facebook and Instagram. These features help users categorize content, discover new posts, and connect with others who share similar interests.

Let's start with talking about Hashtags (#).

A real-life example of successful hashtag usage is Coca-Cola's #ShareACoke campaign. The company encouraged users to share photos of themselves enjoying Coca-Cola products with personalized labels, using the hashtag #ShareACoke. This campaign not only generated significant user-generated content but also fostered a sense of community among Coca-Cola fans.

Let's say you are a fitness coach, if you post a workout video, you might use hashtags like #FitnessGoals and #WorkoutInspiration to reach people interested in fitness. Creating your own branded hashtags can help build your community, like Nike's successful #JustDoIt campaign, which encouraged users to share their fitness achievements under the same hashtag.

Hashtags and tagging are indeed essential tools for expanding your reach on Facebook and Instagram. These features help users categorize content, discover new posts, and connect with others who share similar interests.

In addition to hashtags, tagging is another powerful feature on Facebook and Instagram that allows users to mention or credit other users in their posts. Tagging can help increase the visibility of your content, as it notifies the tagged individual or business and often appears on their profile, potentially reaching their followers as well. For example, a clothing brand might tag a popular fashion influencer wearing their products, increasing the likelihood that the influencer's followers will discover and engage with the brand.

When using hashtags and tagging, it's essential to keep a few best practices in mind. First, always use relevant and specific keywords or phrases that accurately represent your content. This will help ensure your posts reach the intended audience and encourage meaningful engagement. For instance, a fitness trainer might use hashtags like #FitnessGoals, #WorkoutTips, and #HealthyLiving to connect with users interested in fitness and wellness.

Second, avoid using excessive hashtags or unrelated keywords. Overloading your posts with hashtags can appear spammy and may deter potential followers. Instead, focus on a few well-chosen, highly relevant hashtags that truly resonate with your content.

For those who don't know.

Tagging someone on Facebook or Instagram is a feature that enhances the social media experience by allowing users to mention or identify another individual within a post, image, or comment. When a user tags another person, they create a direct link to the mentioned person's profile, making it easier for others to discover and engage with the tagged individual. This feature has various purposes and can benefit both the user and their audience.

One of the primary reasons to tag someone in a post or an image is to notify the tagged individual that they have been mentioned or are visible in the content. For example, during the 2014 Oscars, Ellen DeGeneres took a famous selfie with several celebrities and tagged them in her post, acknowledging their presence and creating a buzz on social media. Tagging helps forge connections between users and encourages interaction, as the tagged person may choose to comment on or share the post.

Tagging can also initiate or contribute to conversations on social media platforms. For instance, when sharing an article about climate change, a user might tag a friend who is passionate about environmental issues, sparking a dialogue and engaging other users in the discussion. This encourages interaction between users and invites the tagged person to share their thoughts or opinions on the subject.

Moreover, tagging can serve as a form of social recommendation. By tagging someone in a post featuring a product, service, or experience, the user implicitly endorses the tagged person's association with the subject matter. For example, if a user visits a new restaurant and posts a picture of their meal while tagging the restaurant, they are effectively recommending it to their followers. This can be especially valuable for businesses, as satisfied customers can share their positive experiences and promote the brand through word-of-mouth marketing.

It is crucial to be considerate and respectful when tagging someone on Facebook or Instagram. Some users may prefer not to be tagged in specific content types or have privacy settings in place to control how they are tagged in posts. Being mindful of these factors ensures that tagging practices contribute positively to the overall social media experience for all involved parties.

Tagging people and brands in your posts, combined with the strategic use of hashtags, can significantly increase visibility and help you reach a broader audience on Facebook and Instagram.

Finally, when tagging other users, always ensure the tag is relevant and adds value to the post. Inappropriate or excessive tagging can be perceived as intrusive and may damage your brand's reputation. For example, a travel blogger might tag a hotel they're staying at or a local tour operator they've collaborated with, but they should avoid tagging unrelated individuals or businesses.

By effectively using hashtags and tagging, you can expand your reach and connect with people who are genuinely interested in your content. This increased visibility can lead to higher engagement, more followers, and ultimately, greater success on social media platforms like Facebook and Instagram.

Hashtags and tagging are powerful tools for increasing your reach on social media. By using relevant keywords and mentioning other users strategically, you can enhance the visibility of your content, connect with a broader audience, and foster a sense of community around shared interests. When utilized effectively, these tools can significantly contribute to the success of an individual or business's social media presence, enabling them to reach new audiences and maintain strong connections with their followers.

You may be wondering to yourself, this is great, but I struggle with coming up with hashtags, how do I find trending hashtags or come up with my own?

One effective approach to finding relevant hashtags involves several steps, including researching popular hashtags in your niche, analyzing competitors' hashtags, using location-based hashtags, creating branded hashtags, and utilizing trending hashtags.

First, research popular hashtags within your niche to discover what's commonly used and resonates with your audience. Tools like Hashtagify, RiteTag, or Keyhole can help you identify these popular hashtags and suggest related ones. For example, a travel blogger might find hashtags like #TravelInspiration and #Wanderlust to be popular among fellow travelers.

Next, analyze the hashtags employed by your competitors to pinpoint the most relevant ones for your niche. Platforms like Sprout Social or Hootsuite can help track your competitors' social media activity and reveal which hashtags they frequently use. Observing your competitors' strategies can give you valuable insights into what works well in your industry.

If your goal is to connect with a local audience, consider incorporating location-based hashtags. These hashtags are specific to a geographic area and can assist in reaching people within that region. Tools like Local Hashtags can help you identify these location-based hashtags for your area. For example, a coffee shop in New York City might use hashtags like #NYCCoffee or #ManhattanCafe to attract local customers.

Creating your own branded hashtags can also help establish your brand identity and make it easier for people to find your content. Branded hashtags can be as straightforward as your brand name or a unique phrase representing your brand. For instance, Coca-Cola's #ShareACoke campaign effectively used a branded hashtag to encourage people to share their experiences with the product.

Finally, taking advantage of trending hashtags can boost your visibility and reach a broader audience. Tools like Twitter Trends, IG Explore, or TikTok Discover can help you identify trending hashtags within your niche. For example, during the holiday season, using hashtags like #HolidayGiftGuide or #ChristmasShopping can help you connect with users looking for seasonal inspiration.

Using relevant hashtags is crucial for social media success. By following the plan outlined above, you can identify hashtags that accurately represent your content and appeal to your target audience. Employing relevant hashtags can enhance your reach, engagement, and overall social media performance.

As we mentioned above, tagging is essential to growing your brand. Even though we've gone into depth about what tagging is, here is a bit more on the strategy behind tagging people.

First, always ensure that you tag relevant people in your posts. The individuals or brands you tag should have a connection to your content or message, as well as your industry. Tagging irrelevant people may result in lower engagement and give off a spammy impression. For instance, if you run a food blog, it would be appropriate to tag a well-known chef in a post discussing their latest cookbook or a particular recipe.

Second, adding a personal touch to your tags can help strengthen relationships and increase engagement. Including a message or comment that is relevant to the person or their brand can foster rapport and encourage conversation. For example, if you're tagging a local artist in a post about their latest exhibition, you could include a comment about your favorite piece or a specific aspect of their work that resonates with you.

Tagging influencers in your posts can also help you gain exposure and extend your reach. Influencers often have a substantial following and can introduce your content to a broader audience. It is crucial, however, to ensure the influencers you tag are relevant to your content or message. A fitness influencer, for instance, might be tagged in a post about a new workout program or a review of fitness equipment.

Collaborating with other brands or individuals in your industry can further expand your reach and increase engagement. When working together, tag the other brand or individual in your posts to enhance their visibility and reach, too. A fashion blogger, for example, could collaborate with a clothing brand for a giveaway, tagging the brand in the promotional post and encouraging their followers to check out the brand's page.

Tagging people effectively is a vital strategy for increasing your social media presence. By tagging relevant people, adding a personal touch, using popular hashtags, tagging influencers, and collaborating with others, you can optimize your social media growth, increase visibility and engagement, and build valuable relationships within your industry.

Chapter 5: Engaging With Your Audience

Engaging with your audience is crucial for increasing your reach on FB and IG. By engaging with your audience, you can build relationships, drive engagement, and reach more people.

Engaging with your audience is a crucial aspect of building a strong online presence and fostering a loyal following. One effective way to accomplish this is by responding to comments on your posts. By taking the time to address your audience's thoughts and concerns, you demonstrate that you genuinely care about their opinions and feedback.

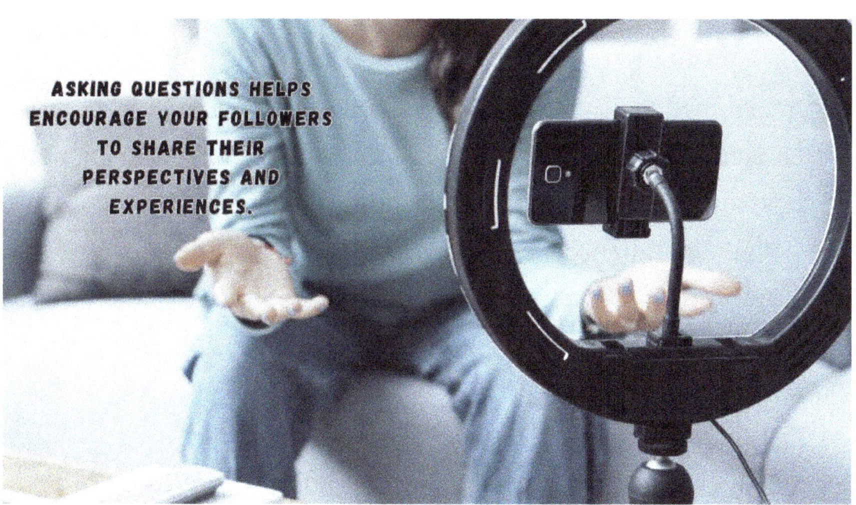

Another strategy to boost engagement is to ask thought-provoking questions. By encouraging your followers to share their perspectives and experiences, you create an interactive environment that fosters genuine connections. This not only strengthens the relationship between you and your audience but also allows you to gain valuable insights into their preferences and needs.

Collaborating with other brands and influencers can also contribute to increased audience engagement. By sharing audiences, you can tap into new demographics, expand your reach, and create a sense of community. Partnering with like-minded individuals or companies can help you grow your brand, broaden your network, and ultimately, boost your overall online presence.

Nurturing audience engagement is essential for any successful online presence. By responding to comments, asking engaging questions, and collaborating with others to share audiences, you can create a thriving community that supports your brand and fosters long-term loyalty.

Social media has revolutionized the way we communicate, connect, and engage with others. It has also allowed businesses and individuals to build their brands, connect with their audience, and engage with them on a personal level. One of the most important aspects of social media engagement is responding to comments.

When you post on social media, it is important to remember that you are not just sharing content, but also engaging with your audience. Responding to comments is a way to show your audience that you care about them and their opinions. Here are some reasons why responding to comments is important:

Increase engagement:

When you respond to comments, it encourages others to engage with your content as well. This can help increase the overall engagement on your post and make it more visible to a wider audience.

Build relationships:

Responding to comments is a way to build relationships with your audience. It shows that you are listening to their opinions, addressing their concerns, and valuing their feedback. This can help you build a loyal following and create a sense of community around your brand.

Encourage feedback:

Responding to comments can also encourage your audience to provide feedback on your content. This can help you understand what your audience likes or dislikes about your content, and make adjustments accordingly.

Improve customer service:

Responding to comments can also be a way to provide customer service. If someone has a question or concern, responding to them in a timely and helpful manner can help you provide better customer service and build trust with your audience.

Continuing to engage with your audience on social media platforms like Facebook and Instagram also allows you to keep up with current trends and adjust your content strategy accordingly. Staying informed about your audience's interests and preferences can help you produce more relevant and engaging content that resonates with them.

Moreover, engaging with your audience can help you identify potential brand advocates or influencers within your community. Recognizing and nurturing these relationships can lead to valuable partnerships, collaborations, or user-generated content that can further enhance your brand's reach and credibility.

Additionally, maintaining active engagement with your audience can also provide valuable insights into your target market's demographics and behaviors. This information can be used to fine-tune your marketing and advertising strategies, ensuring that your efforts are better aligned with your audience's needs and interests.

Consistent engagement with your audience also allows you to monitor and address any negative feedback or potential issues promptly. By proactively addressing concerns or criticisms, you demonstrate your commitment to customer satisfaction and can potentially turn negative experiences into positive ones, ultimately protecting your brand's reputation.

Another essential aspect of engaging with your audience is asking questions. By posing thought-provoking questions related to your content or industry, you encourage your followers to share their thoughts, opinions, and experiences. This not only increases engagement on your posts but also fosters a sense of community among your audience.

For instance, a fitness blogger might ask their followers about their favorite workout routines or tips for staying motivated. By posing such questions, the blogger not only increases engagement on their posts but also gains valuable insights into their audience's preferences, which can help inform future content.

Collaborating with other brands and influencers can also significantly expand your reach and help you connect with new audiences. By partnering with like-minded individuals or businesses, you can create unique content that appeals to both your existing audience and the new audience of your collaborator.

For example, a small coffee shop might collaborate with a local bakery to offer exclusive pastry and coffee pairings. Both the coffee shop and bakery could promote this partnership on their respective social media accounts, exposing each business to the other's audience and potentially attracting new customers.

Effectively engaging with your audience on social media platforms such as Facebook and Instagram is vital for building relationships, driving engagement, and reaching more people. By responding to comments, asking questions, and collaborating with other brands and influencers, you can create a strong, loyal community around your brand and ultimately achieve greater success on social media.

Engaging with your audience is of paramount importance, and one of the most effective ways to do so is by responding to comments on your social media platforms. When done correctly, this can help you build a strong relationship with your audience, foster a sense of community around your brand, and improve your customer service. In this section of the ebook, we'll delve into the art of responding to comments effectively, as well as share some practical tips and real-life examples to inspire you.

First and foremost, it's essential to respond to comments promptly. Your audience will appreciate the timely attention you give to their thoughts and opinions, which demonstrates your commitment to active engagement on your social media platforms. For example, consider a scenario where a potential customer has a question about your product. If you address their query within a few hours, it not only shows that you are attentive to their needs but also increases the likelihood of a sale. In contrast, a delayed response may result in the loss of that customer to a competitor.

Secondly, be genuine and authentic when responding to comments. Your audience can easily detect insincerity or canned responses, which may negatively impact your brand image. So, make an effort to personalize your replies and show that you genuinely care about your audience's opinions and experiences. For instance, if a customer compliments your product, take the time to thank them and ask about their favorite features. This level of engagement will help you build trust and create a sense of community around your brand.

Addressing concerns is another crucial aspect of responding to comments effectively. It's inevitable that at some point, someone will express dissatisfaction or raise an issue regarding your product or service. How you handle these situations can make or break your brand's reputation. When faced with a complaint or concern, always respond professionally and helpfully. Take the time to understand the problem, express empathy, and offer a solution.

A real-life example of this can be found in the way that Amazon handles customer complaints. When a customer expressed disappointment with a product they received (if fulfilled by Amazon), the retailer promptly replies to the comment, apologized for the inconvenience, and offers a full refund or replacement in many cases. This approach not only resolved the customer's issue but also showcased the brand's commitment to exceptional customer service.

Responding to comments is an essential aspect of effective audience engagement. By responding promptly, being genuine, and addressing concerns professionally, you can create a strong sense of community around your brand, build trust with your audience, and enhance your customer service. Keep these principles in mind as you navigate the world of social media and watch your brand flourish as a result.

Showing appreciation is another key aspect of engaging with your audience through comments. When someone compliments your content or shares a positive experience with your brand, don't miss the opportunity to express gratitude. A simple "thank you" can go a long way in building a positive relationship with your audience and encouraging them to continue engaging with your content in the future. For example, if someone praises your blog post for its insightful information, respond with a heartfelt thank you and mention that you're glad they found it helpful. This small gesture can create a lasting impression on your audience and foster loyalty to your brand.

Encouraging further engagement is an excellent way to deepen your connection with your audience and keep them interested in your content. When responding to comments, consider asking open-ended questions, inviting feedback, or suggesting related content that they might find valuable. By doing so, you create a two-way conversation, allowing your audience to feel heard and valued. For instance, if a customer comments on a post about a new product, you might ask them what other products they'd like to see in your lineup or invite them to share their thoughts on the new offering after they've tried it. This strategy encourages your audience to become more invested in your brand and its offerings.

Responding to comments on your social media posts is a vital component of a successful social media strategy. By responding promptly, being genuine, addressing concerns, showing appreciation, and encouraging further engagement, you can cultivate meaningful relationships with your audience, enhance your customer service, and foster a sense of community around your brand. Consistently engaging with your audience through comments demonstrates that you truly care about their opinions and value their feedback, which in turn will contribute to the growth and success of your brand in the long run.

Another great way of engaging your audience is by asking them questions. Asking questions is a powerful way to engage your audience and foster meaningful interactions. By posing questions to your audience, you can glean valuable insights into their interests, preferences, and opinions, all of which can help inform your future content and marketing strategies. Let's take a closer look at the benefits of asking questions and how they can contribute to the growth and success of your brand, with real-life examples to illustrate their impact.

Increasing engagement is a primary reason to incorporate questions into your social media strategy. When you ask questions, you invite your audience to interact with your content, leading to more likes, comments, and shares. A prime example of this can be seen on the social media page of a popular fitness brand. They often pose questions to their followers, such as, "What's your favorite way to stay active during the winter months?" This encourages their audience to engage with the post, share their experiences, and connect with others who share their interests.

Another benefit of asking questions is that it encourages feedback from your audience. Understanding what your audience likes or dislikes about your content enables you to make data-driven adjustments to better resonate with them. For instance, a renowned chef may ask her Instagram followers which recipes they'd like to see her create next. By doing so, she can tailor her future content to align with her audience's preferences and maintain their interest.

Building relationships with your audience is crucial for long-term success, and asking questions can facilitate this process. By showing that you care about their opinions and value their feedback, you can create a loyal following and foster a sense of community around your brand. A local coffee shop, for example, may ask their Facebook followers about their favorite coffee blends or brewing methods. This not only encourages conversation and engagement but also helps the coffee shop connect with its customers on a more personal level.

Lastly, asking questions can serve as a wellspring of ideas for future content. By learning about your audience's interests and preferences, you can craft content that resonates with them and drives further engagement. A travel blogger, for example, might ask their audience which destinations they'd like to see covered in upcoming blog posts. This information can then be used to create content that caters directly to their audience's desires, ensuring that their content remains relevant and appealing.

Asking questions is an essential tool for driving engagement, encouraging feedback, building relationships, and generating ideas for future content. By incorporating questions into your social media strategy, you can foster deeper connections with your audience, better understand their needs and interests, and create content that resonates with them, ultimately contributing to the growth and success of your brand.

Asking effective questions is an art in itself, and mastering this skill can significantly boost your audience engagement and brand growth. In this section, we'll delve into the best practices for asking questions that elicit meaningful responses and foster strong connections with your audience. Real-life examples will be used to demonstrate how these practices can be implemented successfully.

Firstly, ensure that your questions are relevant to your content, industry, or overarching message. By doing so, you will attract more meaningful responses and maintain a focused conversation. For example, a fashion brand could ask its Instagram followers which upcoming trends they are most excited about. This question is directly related to the industry and encourages followers to share their thoughts and opinions on a topic that is likely to interest them.

Keeping your questions simple and easy to answer is another key to success. Complicated or multi-part questions may deter people from responding, so aim for clarity and brevity. A yoga instructor, for instance, could ask their Facebook followers, "What's your favorite yoga pose for relaxation?" This straightforward question encourages engagement by allowing followers to quickly and easily share their preferences.

Using visuals, such as images or videos, can make your questions more engaging and eye-catching, which can lead to increased responses and overall engagement. For example, a travel agency might share a stunning photo of two different beach destinations on their Instagram page and ask their followers, "Which beach would you rather visit: A or B?" The visually appealing post is likely to capture the attention of the audience and encourage them to participate in the conversation.

Following up with those who respond to your questions is crucial for fostering a sense of engagement and building relationships with your audience. By replying to comments or engaging in conversation, you demonstrate that you genuinely care about their input. For instance, when a skincare company asks their Twitter followers about their favorite skincare routines, they should make an effort to respond to each comment, expressing gratitude for the input and perhaps even sharing tips or suggestions.

Lastly, using polls can be an effective way to ask questions on social media. Polls are quick, easy to answer, and provide valuable insights into your audience's preferences and opinions. A restaurant, for example, could create a Twitter poll asking customers to vote for their favorite menu item. The results can not only inform future menu decisions but also generate buzz and excitement around the restaurant's offerings.

Asking effective questions is an essential skill for driving audience engagement and building strong relationships. By keeping your questions relevant, simple, visually appealing, and engaging, you can create an environment in which your audience feels valued and heard. Utilizing polls and following up with those who respond further enhances this connection, ultimately contributing to the growth and success of your brand.

With the development of new social media platforms and new features, there are always new and innovative ways to interact with your audience. Keeping up with new features is essential to keep connected with your audience! Another great way to connect with not only your audience but with other people's audience, allowing you to grow your audience, is by collaborating with other creators.

Collaborating with other brands and influencers is an effective way to broaden your reach, engage with new audiences, and strengthen your brand's online presence. By working together with like-minded individuals or businesses, you can create unique opportunities for growth and exposure. In this section, we'll explore the benefits of collaboration, along with real-life examples that demonstrate its potential impact.

Reaching new audiences is one of the primary reasons to collaborate with other brands and influencers. By working together, you can expose your brand to new followers who may not have previously encountered your content. For example, a fitness apparel company might collaborate with a popular fitness influencer for a joint workout challenge, which could attract the influencer's followers to the apparel brand's social media pages, resulting in increased visibility, engagement, and potential new customers.

Building relationships is another important aspect of collaboration. As you work together with other brands and influencers, you'll forge valuable connections that can pave the way for future collaborations or partnerships. Moreover, these relationships can help create a sense of community around your brand. A real-life example of this can be found in the beauty industry, where makeup brands frequently collaborate with well-known makeup artists or beauty influencers. These partnerships not only create buzz around the brand but also foster a sense of camaraderie among fans of both parties.

Creating unique content is a significant benefit of collaborating with others. By joining forces, you can produce engaging and distinctive content that sets your brand apart from the competition. For instance, a home decor brand might team up with a popular interior designer to create a series of exclusive design tips and DIY projects for their social media followers. This innovative content can help increase engagement and solidify the brand's identity.

Increasing credibility is another advantage of collaboration. By partnering with respected brands and influencers in your industry, you can establish trust and credibility among your target audience. A prime example of this can be seen in the technology sector, where established tech companies often collaborate with up-and- coming startups. This association with a reputable brand can help the startup gain credibility, while the established company benefits from the innovative ideas and fresh perspective of the newcomer.

Collaborating with other brands and influencers is a powerful strategy for expanding your reach, engaging with new audiences, and enhancing your social media presence. By focusing on reaching new audiences, building relationships, creating unique content, and increasing credibility, you can successfully leverage collaboration to bolster your brand's reputation and growth. Be open to forging partnerships with others in your industry, and embrace the opportunities that collaboration can bring.

Collaborating with other brands and influencers offers a wealth of advantages that can significantly boost your brand's online presence and overall growth. By working hand- in-hand with like-minded individuals or businesses, you can create distinctive opportunities for increased exposure and engagement. In this section, we'll delve deeper into the advantages of collaboration and provide real-life examples that showcase its potential impact.

Expanding your reach and tapping into new audiences is a crucial reason for collaborating with other brands and influencers. By joining forces, you can introduce your brand to an entirely new set of followers who may not have encountered your content before. For example, a sustainable fashion brand could collaborate with an eco-conscious lifestyle blogger for a joint campaign, drawing the blogger's audience to the brand's social media pages and potentially converting them into customers.

Fostering relationships is another essential aspect of collaboration. As you collaborate with other brands and influencers, you build valuable connections that can lead to future collaborations or partnerships. Furthermore, these relationships can help cultivate a sense of community around your brand. A real-life example of this can be seen in the podcasting world, where podcast hosts often invite guests from other podcasts in the same niche. This cross-promotion not only generates excitement among fans of both shows but also nurtures a sense of unity and shared interests.

Creating exclusive content is a considerable advantage of collaborating with others. You can generate captivating content that distinguishes your brand from competitors by pooling resources and expertise. For example, an organic food company might partner with a well-known nutritionist to develop a collection of healthy recipes exclusively for their social media followers. This one-of-a-kind content can boost engagement and strengthen the brand's image.

Boosting credibility is yet another benefit of collaboration. By teaming up with esteemed brands and influencers in your sector, you can earn trust and credibility with your target audience. A great example of this can be seen in the automotive industry, where luxury car manufacturers sometimes collaborate with high-end fashion brands to create limited-edition vehicles. This partnership enhances the credibility and desirability of both brands, while also generating buzz among their respective fan bases.

Collaboration with other brands and influencers is a potent strategy for growing your reach, engaging new audiences, and amplifying your social media presence. By concentrating on expanding your audience, nurturing relationships, producing exclusive content, and bolstering credibility, you can effectively leverage collaboration to enhance your brand's reputation and growth. Remain open to forming partnerships with others in your field and seize the opportunities that collaboration can offer.

Chapter 6: Utilizing Facebook and IG Ads

Facebook and Instagram offer an array of advertising options that can help you reach your target audience and expand your reach. Effectively utilizing Facebook and Instagram Ads requires careful planning and execution. In this section, we will outline key aspects of successful ad campaigns.

Setting clear objectives is vital for creating effective Facebook and Instagram ads. Defining your goals allows you to measure the success of your campaign, target your ads effectively, and create cost-effective ads that deliver optimal results. For example, a small online clothing store may set a specific goal of increasing website traffic by 20% within one month through a carefully designed ad campaign. By having a measurable objective, the store can track its progress and make adjustments as needed.

Targeting your audience is another crucial aspect of running successful ads on Facebook and Instagram. Utilizing the platforms' advanced targeting options enables you to reach the right audience and create ads that resonate with them. A real-life example of this can be seen in a local gym that uses Facebook and Instagram's location-based targeting to reach potential customers in their area, offering them a special promotion to join the gym.

Using eye-catching images and videos in your ads is essential for capturing your audience's attention. High-quality visuals can make your ads stand out and encourage users to engage with your content. For instance, a travel agency might use stunning images and video footage of a tropical destination to promote their vacation packages, enticing viewers to learn more and potentially book a trip.

Testing and refining your ads is a vital component of a successful ad campaign. By monitoring your ads' performance, you can identify what's working and what needs improvement, allowing you to optimize your strategy. A real-life example of this is a restaurant that tests different ad creatives and headlines to determine which combination results in the highest number of reservations. Based on this data, the restaurant can refine its ads to maximize its effectiveness.

Meta Business ads on Facebook and Instagram are an incredibly powerful tool for reaching your target audience and achieving your marketing objectives. By setting clear objectives, targeting your audience effectively, using eye-catching visuals, and continually testing and refining your ads, you can create engaging and impactful ads that resonate with your target audience. Remember that successful ad campaigns require ongoing monitoring and optimization, so always be prepared to adapt and improve your strategy to achieve the best possible results.

As you continue to leverage Facebook and Instagram Ads to achieve your marketing goals, it's essential to stay updated on new features and best practices. In this section, we'll discuss additional considerations and strategies to help you make the most of your advertising efforts on these platforms.

Utilize various ad formats:

Facebook and Instagram offer multiple ad formats, such as image ads, video ads, carousel ads, and story ads. Each format serves a different purpose and can cater to different objectives. For example, a non-profit organization might use a video ad to share a compelling story about the impact of their work, whereas a retail brand might use a carousel ad to showcase a selection of products.

Leverage custom audiences and lookalike audiences:

Custom audiences allow you to target people who have already interacted with your business, while lookalike audiences help you reach new users who are similar to your existing customers. For instance, an online bookstore could create a custom audience of users who visited their website in the past month and target them with ads featuring personalized book recommendations. The bookstore could also use a lookalike audience to reach potential new customers with similar reading interests.

Monitor ad performance and adjust bidding strategies:

Keeping track of your ads' performance is crucial for optimizing your campaign's return on investment (ROI). Adjusting your bidding strategies based on the performance data can help you achieve better results. For example, a software company might increase its bid for ads targeting users who have previously downloaded their free trial, as these users are more likely to convert into paying customers.

Experiment with retargeting campaigns:

Retargeting campaigns are designed to re-engage users who have already interacted with your brand but haven't completed a desired action, such as making a purchase. A real-life example of this is an e-commerce website running a retargeting campaign to show ads featuring products that users have previously viewed but not purchased, encouraging them to reconsider and complete their purchase.

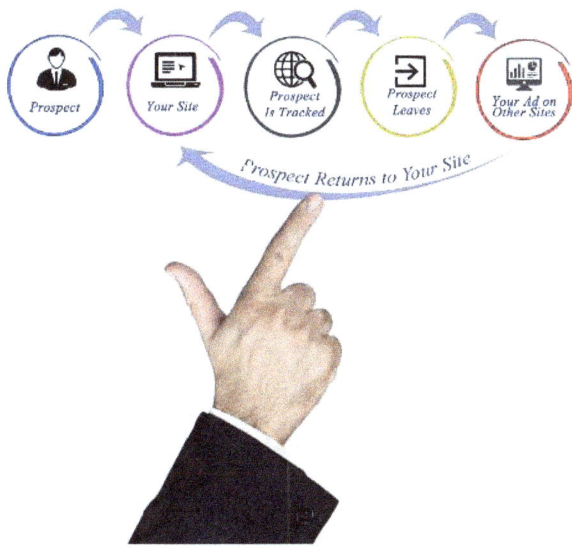

By utilizing various ad formats, leveraging custom and lookalike audiences, monitoring ad performance, adjusting bidding strategies, and experimenting with retargeting campaigns, you can further enhance the effectiveness of your Facebook and Instagram Ads. Always stay informed about the latest developments and best practices in social media advertising to ensure your campaigns remain relevant, engaging, and successful. Remember, success in social media advertising requires continuous learning, adaptation, and improvement, so keep refining your strategy and exploring new growth opportunities.

One of the most important ways to improve your advertising on social media is through targeted ads.

Choosing the right targeting options is crucial for successfully reaching your desired audience on Facebook and Instagram. By making use of the platform's advanced targeting options, you can create highly personalized and relevant ads that appeal to your audience based on their interests, demographics, behaviors, and similarities to existing customers. In this section, we will explore the importance of targeted advertising and provide real-life examples to illustrate its impact.

Using Facebook and Instagram's targeting options effectively enables you to create ads that resonate with your audience, leading to increased engagement. For example, a local coffee shop might use demographic targeting to reach potential customers within a specific age range and location, ensuring that their ads are seen by users who are most likely to visit the shop. Additionally, they could use interest-based targeting to reach users who have expressed a love for specialty coffee, further refining their audience and increasing the likelihood of engagement.

Testing and optimizing your targeting options is essential for improving the performance of your ads. Utilizing Facebook and Instagram's analytics tools allows you to track your results and make necessary adjustments to your targeting strategy. A real-life example of this could be a sports apparel brand that initially targets its ads based on general sports interests. After analyzing their ad performance data, they may discover that users interested in specific sports, such as running or yoga, engage more with their ads. The brand can then refine its targeting options to focus on these niche interests, resulting in improved ad performance.

Targeted advertising is a highly effective way to connect with your audience on Facebook and Instagram. By defining your audience, choosing the appropriate targeting options, and continually testing and optimizing your ads, you can achieve remarkable success on these platforms. Always be prepared to analyze and adjust your strategy based on performance data, and don't hesitate to explore new targeting options to reach an even more relevant audience. By doing so, you can ensure that your ads consistently resonate with your target audience, ultimately driving engagement and achieving your marketing objectives.

Using eye-catching images and videos in your ads is crucial to capturing your audience's attention. High-quality visuals can make all the difference in setting your ads apart from the rest. In this section, we will explore tips for using captivating images and videos, along with real-life examples that showcase the power of visually appealing ads.

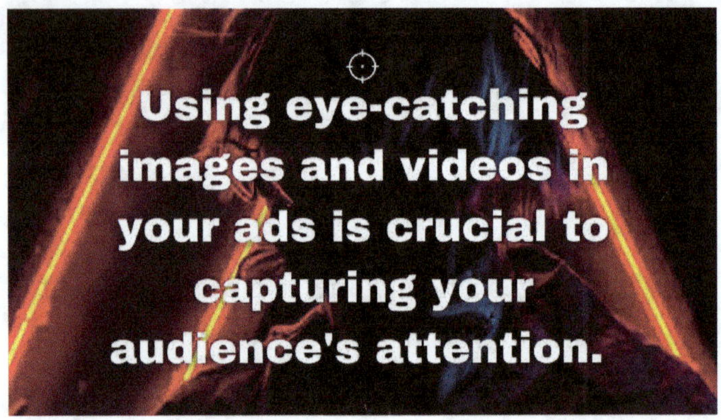

High-quality images are essential for grabbing your audience's attention. Clear, crisp, and visually appealing photos are more likely to draw in users as they scroll through their social media feeds. For example, an online clothing store might use high- resolution images of their products on models, showcasing the vibrant colors and textures of their garments. By presenting visually appealing images, the brand can capture the interest of potential customers and encourage them to explore its offerings further.

Visually appealing videos can also serve as powerful attention-grabbers in your ads. Engaging, informative, and visually stimulating videos can pique the curiosity of your audience and encourage them to learn more about your brand. For instance, a travel agency might use captivating videos showcasing breathtaking destinations or exciting adventures, enticing viewers to consider booking a trip. By incorporating captions, the agency can ensure its videos are accessible to a wider audience, including those who watch with the sound off.

Keeping your images and videos simple is important to convey your message effectively. Avoid cluttered visuals or complex videos that may be difficult for your audience to understand. For example, a fitness brand might use clean, minimalist images or videos that demonstrate specific exercises or techniques. This straightforward approach ensures that the brand's message is easily understood and encourages users to engage with the content.

A clear call-to-action (CTA) is essential for guiding your audience toward a specific action, such as visiting your website or landing page. For example, a software company might use a "Learn More" button in their ad, directing viewers to a page where they can explore the features and benefits of their product. By incorporating a clear CTA, the company can drive traffic to its website and potentially generate new leads.

Testing and optimizing your images and videos are crucial for improving the performance of your ads. By utilizing Facebook and Instagram's analytics tools, you can track your results and make adjustments to your visuals as needed. For example, a food delivery service might test several different images featuring various meal options, then analyze the performance data to determine which images resonate most with their audience. By optimizing their visuals based on this data, the service can create more effective ads that drive engagement and conversions.

Using eye-catching images and videos in your social media ads is essential for standing out in a crowded advertising landscape. By employing high-quality visuals, keeping your content simple, incorporating clear CTAs, and continuously testing and optimizing your ads, you can create captivating and effective ads that grab your audience's attention and encourage them to engage with your brand.

Now that you have created your ad it may still need to be optimized, Many times ads have to go through multiple iterations until it is a perfect ad. Even if an ad is successful, testing multiple versions of your ad is essential to help increase your conversion rate. Testing and refining your ads can help you create more effective campaigns that resonate with your target audience.

Setting clear goals is the first step in testing and refining your ads. For example, a local bakery might set a goal to increase brand awareness within their community and drive foot traffic to their store. By establishing clear objectives, the bakery can measure the success of its ad campaigns and make necessary adjustments.

Creating multiple ad variations allows you to test which ads perform better and optimize your campaign accordingly. For instance, an online tutoring service might create several ad variations featuring different subject offerings, images, and headlines. By testing these variations, the service can determine which ads resonate most with their audience and drive more sign-ups.

Testing your ads and tracking their performance is crucial for identifying what works and what doesn't. For example, a subscription box service might test different ad formats, such as static images, carousel ads, and video ads. Using Facebook and Instagram's analytics tools, the service can analyze the performance of each ad format and optimize their campaign based on the results.

Refining your strategy based on the insights gained from testing is essential for creating more effective ads. For example, a software company might discover that ads featuring customer testimonials perform better than those showcasing product features. The company can then adjust its strategy to incorporate more testimonials into its ads, increasing its chances of success.

Continuous testing and refining of your ads will ensure that your ad campaigns stay relevant and effective. For example, a fitness studio might regularly test new ad variations with seasonal promotions, updated class schedules, or new instructors. By continually refining its ad strategy based on the latest data, the studio can optimize its campaigns and achieve its marketing goals.

Testing and refining your ads is a critical component of creating effective Facebook and Instagram ad campaigns. By setting clear goals, creating multiple ad variations, testing your ads, identifying what's working, refining your strategy, and testing again, you can optimize your ad campaigns and accomplish your marketing objectives. Continuously test and refine your ads to stay ahead in the competitive world of social media advertising.

Chapter 7: Measuring Your Success

Measuring your success on Facebook and Instagram is crucial for determining the effectiveness of your strategies for increasing reach. By tracking key metrics and analyzing audience insights, you can refine your approach and drive better results. In this section, we will discuss how to measure your success and provide real-life examples that illustrate the importance of tracking your progress.

Tracking engagement on your posts helps you understand what content resonates with your audience. For example, a photography business might track the number of likes, comments, and shares on its posts to determine which types of images or techniques generate the most interest. By analyzing this data, the business can focus on creating content that their audience finds valuable and engaging.

Monitoring your reach enables you to gauge how many people are seeing your content. For instance, a local coffee shop might track the organic and paid reach of its posts to assess the effectiveness of its content strategy and advertising efforts. By monitoring reach, the coffee shop can identify trends and make data-driven decisions to expand its audience.

Using Facebook and Instagram's Audience Insights can help you better understand your audience and tailor your content to their preferences. For example, a sports equipment retailer might analyze their audience's demographics, interests, and online behaviors to create targeted campaigns that appeal to its customer base. By leveraging audience insights, the retailer can develop more effective strategies for reaching and engaging their target audience.

Setting clear goals and tracking your progress are essential for measuring your success on social media. For example, an eco-friendly cosmetics company might set a goal to increase brand awareness and track key metrics such as engagement, reach, and website traffic. By monitoring these metrics, the company can assess its performance and make adjustments to its strategy as needed.

Measuring your success on Facebook and Instagram is critical for optimizing your strategies and achieving your marketing goals. By tracking engagement, monitoring reach, analyzing audience insights, and setting and tracking goals, you can gain valuable insights into your performance and make data-driven decisions to improve your results. Continuously evaluate your efforts to ensure that your strategies are effective and driving the desired outcomes on social media platforms.

Analyze Post Performance:

Regularly review the performance of individual posts to determine which types of content generate the most engagement. For example, a travel agency might analyze the likes, comments, and shares on posts featuring various destinations or travel tips to understand which topics resonate most with their audience. By identifying the high-performing content, the agency can focus on creating similar posts to boost engagement.

Track Engagement Over Time:

Monitor your engagement metrics over time to identify patterns and trends. For example, a restaurant might track its engagement every month, looking for any fluctuations or growth in likes, comments, and shares. By analyzing these trends, the restaurant can adjust its content strategy or posting schedule to optimize engagement.

Benchmark Against Competitors:

Compare your engagement metrics to those of your competitors to gauge how well your content is resonating with your audience. For instance, a fashion brand might analyze the engagement rates of similar brands on Facebook and Instagram to determine if their content is performing well within their industry. By benchmarking against competitors, you can identify areas of strength and weakness, and adjust your strategy accordingly.

Engage with Your Audience:

Actively engage with your audience by responding to comments and messages on your social media platforms. This not only helps foster a sense of community around your brand but also provides valuable insights into your audience's preferences and opinions. For example, fitness influencers might reply to comments and questions on their posts, using the feedback to tailor their content and better serve their followers' needs.

Leverage Third-Party Analytics Tools:

In addition to Facebook and Instagram Insights, consider using third-party analytics tools to gain deeper insights into your engagement metrics. These tools can help you analyze and visualize your data in more detail, allowing you to make informed decisions about your content strategy.

Tracking your engagement on Facebook and Instagram is crucial for evaluating the success of your social media marketing efforts and making data-driven decisions to optimize your strategy. By using Facebook and Instagram Insights, analyzing post- performance, monitoring engagement over time, benchmarking against competitors, engaging with your audience, and leveraging third-party analytics tools, you can gain valuable insights into your performance and make informed decisions to improve your results.

Track your reach and impressions:

For example, a local coffee shop may monitor its reach and impressions on Facebook and Instagram to understand how well its content is being seen by potential customers. By analyzing these metrics, the coffee shop can adjust its ad targeting, content strategy, or posting schedule to increase its visibility and ultimately drive more foot traffic.

Monitor your engagement rate:

A cosmetics brand may track its engagement rate to determine which types of content are generating the most interest from its target audience. If tutorial videos have a higher engagement rate than product photos, the brand can prioritize creating more tutorial content to better serve its audience and drive sales.

Monitor your follower growth:

A tech startup might track its follower growth on Facebook and Instagram to measure the success of its content strategy and brand awareness efforts. A steady increase in followers may indicate that the startup's content is resonating with its target audience, while a plateau or decline may signal a need for a change in strategy.

Keep an eye on your competition:

An online fitness platform may monitor its competitors' performance on social media to identify trends, best practices, and areas for improvement. For example, if a competitor sees success with live workout sessions, the fitness platform may consider incorporating live sessions into its content strategy to boost engagement and attract new users.

Measuring the effectiveness of your strategies for increasing your reach on Facebook and Instagram is crucial for refining your approach and achieving your marketing goals. By tracking your reach, impressions, engagement rate, and follower growth, and monitoring your competition, you can gain valuable insights into your performance, identify areas for improvement, and make data-driven decisions to optimize your social media marketing efforts.

Establish SMART goals:

Ensure that your goals are Specific, Measurable, Achievable, Relevant, and Time- bound (SMART). This will help you create clear and actionable goals that can be effectively tracked and assessed.

Break down your goals into smaller milestones:

Breaking down your goals into smaller milestones makes them more manageable and allows you to track your progress more effectively. This also helps you stay motivated and focused as you work toward achieving your larger objectives.

Align your goals with your overall marketing strategy:

Ensure that your FB and IG goals align with your overall marketing strategy, as this will help you create a cohesive and consistent brand message across all marketing channels.

Assign KPIs to track your goals:

Assign Key Performance Indicators (KPIs) to each goal to help you measure your progress. KPIs can include metrics like engagement rate, click-through rate, conversions, or return on ad spend (ROAS).

Regularly review and adjust your goals:

Regularly review your goals and track your progress to ensure you're on track to achieve them. Adjust your goals as needed based on your performance and any changes in your business or marketing strategy.

A startup tech company may define its objectives on FB and IG as increasing brand awareness, attracting potential investors, and driving website traffic to showcase its innovative product offerings.

Establish SMART goals:

An e-commerce clothing store might set a SMART goal to increase its Instagram followers by 20% within the next three months, using a combination of organic content and paid advertising.

Break down your goals into smaller milestones:

A local coffee shop could break down its goal of generating 100 new leads through Facebook ads into smaller milestones, such as generating 25 new leads per week for four weeks.

Align your goals with your overall marketing strategy:

A travel agency might align its FB and IG goals with its overall marketing strategy by focusing on promoting specific travel packages, targeting demographics that align with its ideal customer profile, and increasing website bookings.

Assign KPIs to track your goals:

A software company aiming to increase its website traffic from Facebook and Instagram could assign KPIs such as click-through rate and the number of new website visitors from social media sources.

Setting clear goals on FB and IG is an essential part of social media marketing. By defining your objectives, establishing SMART goals, breaking down goals into smaller milestones, aligning your goals with your overall marketing strategy, and assigning KPIs to track your progress, you can optimize your performance and achieve your marketing goals. Remember to regularly review and adjust your goals as needed to stay on track and respond to any changes in your business or marketing environment.

In conclusion, this eBook has provided you with comprehensive knowledge and practical strategies to navigate the complex yet rewarding world of Facebook and Instagram marketing. By understanding the ins and outs of these powerful social media platforms, you are now equipped with the tools and insights needed to harness their potential and achieve your marketing goals.

Throughout this guide, we have explored essential aspects of social media marketing on Facebook and Instagram, such as audience targeting, ad creation, content optimization, and performance measurement. We have also shared real-life examples and actionable tips that can be applied to various business scenarios, helping you create effective and engaging campaigns that resonate with your audience.

As you move forward with your Facebook and Instagram marketing efforts, remember that the digital landscape is constantly evolving. To stay ahead of the curve, it is crucial to remain adaptable and receptive to new trends, features, and best practices. Regularly review and analyze your performance data, and don't be afraid to experiment with different strategies and creative approaches. By doing so, you can continue to refine your marketing campaigns and maximize your return on investment.

Finally, we hope that this eBook serves as a valuable resource for you as you embark on your journey to social media success. By applying the principles and techniques outlined in this guide, you can unlock the true potential of Facebook and Instagram marketing and drive meaningful results for your business. Good luck, and happy marketing!